DOWNSIDE OF DRUGS

Over-the-Counter Medications

DOWNSIDE OF DRUGS

ADHD Medication Abuse: Ritalin®, Adderall®, & Other Addictive Stimulants

Alcohol & Tobacco

Caffeine: Energy Drinks, Coffee, Soda, & Pills

Dangerous Depressants & Sedatives

Doping: Human Growth Hormone, Steroids, & Other Performance-Enhancing Drugs

Hard Drugs: Cocaine, LSD, PCP, & Heroin

Marijuana: Legal & Developmental Consequences

Methamphetamine & Other Amphetamines

New Drugs: Bath Salts, Spice, Salvia, & Designer Drugs

Over-the-Counter Medications

Prescription Painkillers: OxyContin®, Percocet®, Vicodin®, & Other Addictive Analgesics

DOWNSIDE OF DRUGS

Over-the-Counter Medications

Summit Free Public Library

Rosa Waters

Mason Crest

Mason Crest
450 Parkway Drive, Suite D
Broomall, PA 19008
www.masoncrest.com

Printed and bound in the United States of America.

First printing
9 8 7 6 5 4 3 2 1

Series ISBN: 978-1-4222-3015-2
ISBN: 978-1-4222-3025-1
ebook ISBN: 978-1-4222-8811-5

Cataloging-in-Publication Data on file with the Library of Congress.

3 9547 00414 7349

Contents

INTRODUCTION

One of the best parts of getting older is the opportunity to make your own choices. As your parents give you more space and you spend more time with friends than family, you are called upon to make more decisions for yourself. Many important decisions that present themselves in the teen years may change your life. The people with whom you are friendly, how much effort you put into school and other activities, and what kinds of experiences you choose for yourself all affect the person you will become as you emerge from being a child into becoming a young adult.

One of the most important decisions you will make is whether or not you use substances like alcohol, marijuana, crystal meth, and cocaine. Even using prescription medicines incorrectly or relying on caffeine to get through your daily life can shape your life today and your future tomorrow. These decisions can impact all the other decisions you make. If you decide to say yes to drug abuse, the impact on your life is usually not a good one!

One suggestion I make to many of my patients is this: think about how you will respond to an offer to use drugs before it happens. In the heat of the moment, particularly if you're feeling some peer pressure, it can be hard to think clearly—so be prepared ahead of time. Thinking about why you don't want to use drugs and how you'll respond if you are asked to use them can make it easier to make a healthy decision when the time comes. Just like practicing a sport makes it easier to play in a big game, having thought about why drugs aren't a good fit for you and exactly what you might say to avoid them can give you the "practice" you need to do what's best for you. It can make a tough situation simpler once it arises.

In addition, talk about drugs with your parents or a trusted adult. This will both give you support and help you clarify your thinking. The decision is still yours to make, but adults can be a good resource. Take advantage of the information and help they can offer you.

Sometimes, young people fall into abusing drugs without really thinking about it ahead of time. It can sometimes be hard to recognize when you're making a decision that might hurt you. You might be with a friend or acquaintance in a situation that feels comfortable. There may be things in your life that are hard, and it could seem like using drugs might make them easier. It's also natural to be curious about new experiences. However, by not making a decision ahead of time, you may be actually making a decision without realizing it, one that will limit your choices in the future.

When someone offers you drugs, there is no flashing sign that says, "Hey, think about what you're doing!" Making a good decision may be harder because the "fun" part happens immediately while the downside—the damage to your brain and the rest of your body—may not be obvious right away. One of the biggest downsides of drugs is that they have long-term effects on your life. They could reduce your educational, career, and relationship opportunities. Drug use often leaves users with more problems than when they started.

Whenever you make a decision, it's important to know all the facts. When it comes to drugs, you'll need answers to questions like these: How do different drugs work? Is there any "safe" way to use drugs? How will drugs hurt my body and my brain? If I don't notice any bad effects right away, does that mean these drugs are safe? Are these drugs addictive? What are the legal consequences of using drugs? This book discusses these questions and helps give you the facts to make good decisions.

Reading this book is a great way to start, but if you still have questions, keep looking for the answers. There is a lot of information on the Internet, but not all of it is reliable. At the back of this book, you'll find a list of more books and good websites for finding out more about this drug. A good website is teens.drugabuse.gov, a site compiled for teens by the National Institute on Drug Abuse (NIDA). This is a reputable federal government agency that researches substance use and how to prevent it. This website does a good job looking at a lot of data and consolidating it into easy-to-understand messages.

What if you are worried you already have a problem with drugs? If that's the case, the best thing to do is talk to your doctor or another trusted adult to help figure out what to do next. They can help you find a place to get treatment.

Drugs have a downside—but as a young adult, you have the power to make decisions for yourself about what's best for you. Use your power wisely!

—*Joshua Borus, MD*

1. WHAT ARE OVER-THE-COUNTER DRUGS?

Over-the-counter (OTC) drugs are medicines you can buy without a *prescription* from a doctor. Some OTC drugs relieve pains and itches. Some prevent or cure diseases, like tooth decay and athlete's foot. Others help manage recurring health problems, like migraine headaches.

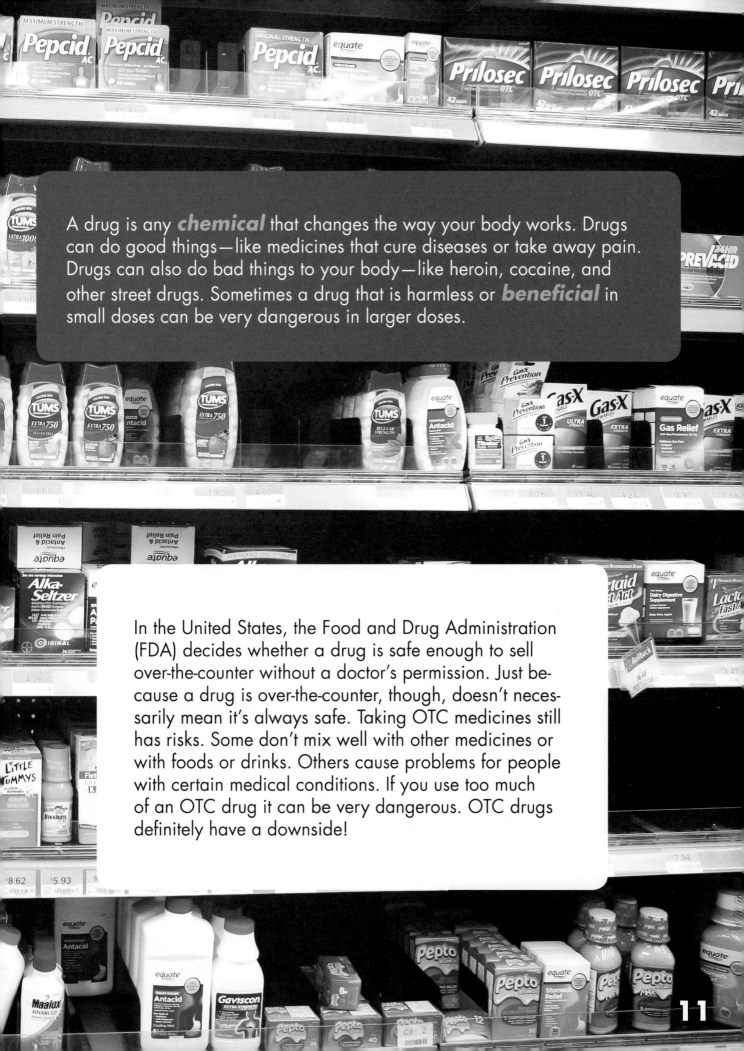

A drug is any *chemical* that changes the way your body works. Drugs can do good things—like medicines that cure diseases or take away pain. Drugs can also do bad things to your body—like heroin, cocaine, and other street drugs. Sometimes a drug that is harmless or *beneficial* in small doses can be very dangerous in larger doses.

In the United States, the Food and Drug Administration (FDA) decides whether a drug is safe enough to sell over-the-counter without a doctor's permission. Just because a drug is over-the-counter, though, doesn't necessarily mean it's always safe. Taking OTC medicines still has risks. Some don't mix well with other medicines or with foods or drinks. Others cause problems for people with certain medical conditions. If you use too much of an OTC drug it can be very dangerous. OTC drugs definitely have a downside!

2. WHAT'S THE DOWNSIDE OF OVER-THE-COUNTER DRUGS?

Lots of people, especially teenagers, think that OTC drugs must be safe since they're legal. But because they're so easy to get, OTC drugs are also easy to abuse. When you take too much of them too often, some OTC drugs can be addictive. Overdoses can damage your body for life. They may even cause death.

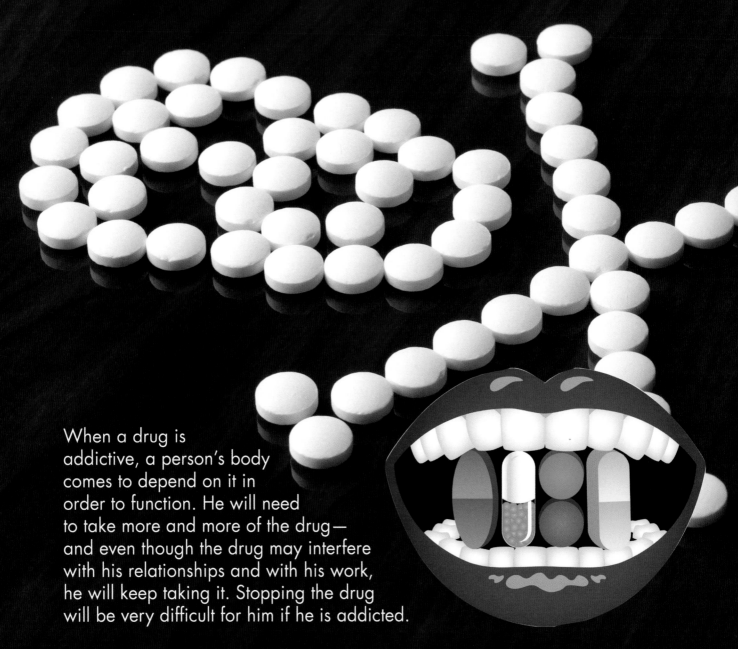

When a drug is addictive, a person's body comes to depend on it in order to function. He will need to take more and more of the drug—and even though the drug may interfere with his relationships and with his work, he will keep taking it. Stopping the drug will be very difficult for him if he is addicted.

The most commonly abused OTC drugs include those that contain the ingredient DXM (dextromethorphan), which is used to treat cough, cold, and flu symptoms.

Other OTC medications that are often abused include those that are intended to help with weight loss—like laxatives, diet pills, and herbal treatments— as well as sleeping pills and Dramamine (a drug that's used to treat motion sickness). All these medications can have serious and even deadly side effects, especially if they're taken over a long time.

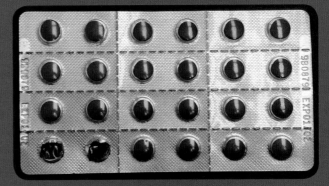

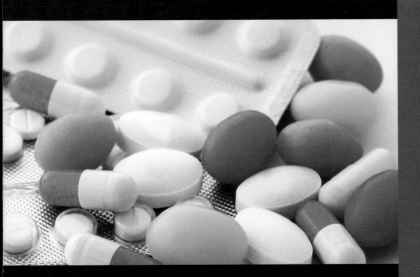

Another OTC drug that can be abused is pseudoephedrine, which is a decongestant. It's used to treat head colds and the stuffiness that comes from allergies—but pseudoephedrine is also a key ingredient used in making the illegal drug methamphetamine.

3. WHAT HAPPENS TO YOUR BODY WHEN YOU USE DXM?

The effects of DXM abuse vary, depending on how much a person takes and what it is combined with. Some people are more *sensitive* to DXM than others.

DXM's short-term effects on a person's body include:

- blurred vision
- slurred speech
- impaired physical coordination
- stomachaches, nausea, and vomiting
- rapid heartbeat
- drowsiness
- numbness of fingers and toes

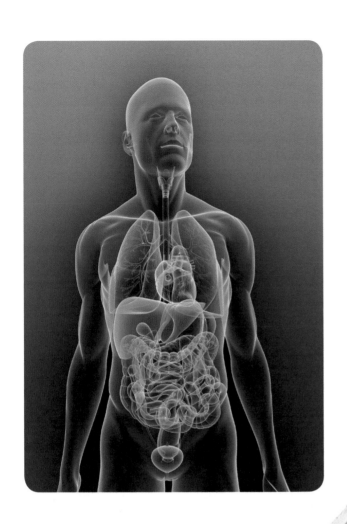

DXM's long-term effects can include liver damage. Cough medications often include acetaminophen along with DXM, which can be very harmful to a person's liver when taken in large quantities.

DXM is very dangerous when combined with alcohol. The combination could kill you! When DXM is combined with antidepressant medications it can also be fatal.

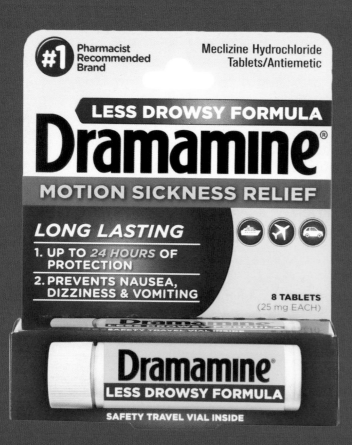

Dramamine is intended to help people cope with motion sickness. It's the brand name for a chemical called dimenhydrinate. It's perfectly safe when it's taken according to the manufacturer's directions—but it becomes dangerous when it's taken in large quantities. And it's even more dangerous if you mix it with alcohol.

Dramamine's short-term effects when taken at the recommended dosage include:

- drowsiness
- dizziness
- blurred vision
- a dry mouth
- clumsiness

The long-term effects can include:

- having no energy
- vomiting
- trouble urinating

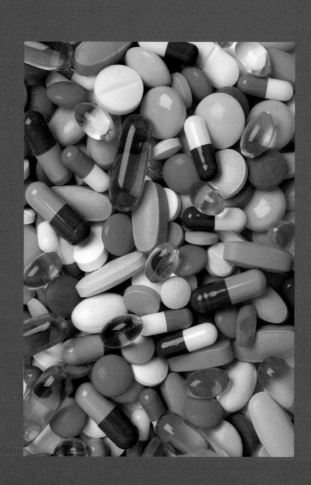

Large doses can cause:

- increased blood pressure and heart rate
- trouble swallowing
- trouble speaking
- trouble breathing
- high fever
- convulsions
- coma

An overdose could kill you. You should get medical attention right away if you've taken an overdose of Dramamine!

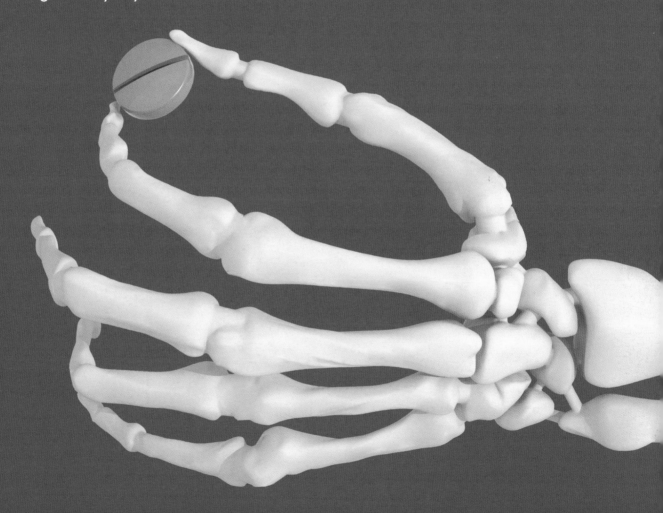

In 2006, a teenager drowned after taking Dramamine mixed with alcohol. The following year, five high-school freshmen landed in the hospital after overdosing on Dramamine.

5. WHAT HAPPENS TO YOUR BODY WHEN YOU USE DIET PILLS?

Diet pills are meant to help people lose weight. In the United States, they don't require approval from the FDA before being sold to the public—so it is easy for unsafe ingredients to find their way into them. Not only do these pills often fail to meet their claims for weight loss, but they can also be dangerous!

Depending on the ingredients, side effects from diet pills can range from:

- increased heart rate
- high blood pressure
- liver damage
- heart problems
- headaches
- nausea and stomach pain
- breathing problems
- addiction

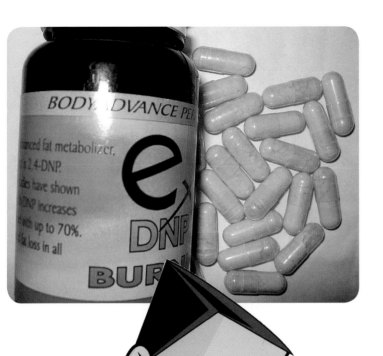

Sometimes, teens also order diet pills off the Internet. These can be deadly. One of these—called DNP—has been responsible for several deaths over the past decade. The pill is intended to keep your body from absorbing fat, but it can cause the body to overheat. The same chemical in DNP is also found in pesticides, which are used to kill insects. It's used in explosives and to develop film as well. It's definitely not something you want inside your body! In September 2013, an eighteen-year-old in Great Britain died after he took DNP.

Some diet pills claim to increase your *metabolism*, so that you burn calories more easily. These pills may also increase your blood pressure and heart rate to dangerous levels. This can cause *stroke* and heart attacks. Laurie Mitan, a doctor at Cincinnati Children's Hospital Medical Center in Ohio, reports: "We've had teens hospitalized in our ICU with [heart problems] after using diet pills just one time!"

If you want to lose weight, a healthy diet and exercise is always the safest—and most effective—route to take!

6. WHAT HAPPENS TO YOUR BODY WHEN YOU USE SLEEPING PILLS?

Most over-the-counter sleep aids contain antihistamines. These are the same drugs often used to treat allergies. They make you drowsy. Everyone has difficulty falling asleep some-times—but OTC sleeping pills should only be taken once in a while. They're not meant to be taken every night. If taken too often, they can become addictive.

Sleeping pills are meant to help you get a good night's sleep—but sometimes, people still feel sleepy the next day. When that happens, they may not be able to drive safely, operate machinery, or think clearly. The sleeping pill they took the night before could cause a fatal accident!

Sleeping pills can also cause these problems:

- stomachaches
- diarrhea or constipation
- dizziness

Mixing OTC sleeping pills and even a little bit of alcohol is very dangerous. Alcohol increases the effects of the sleeping pills.

If you become addicted to OTC sleep aids, when you try to stop taking them, your sleep problem will be even worse than it was before. You may also have serious *withdrawal* symptoms that include shakiness, sweating, and nausea.

Pseudoephedrine can be used to make methamphetamine (meth), a very dangerous *illicit* drug. This is probably the most well-known way this drug is misused. However, it can also be abused by taking it for any reason other than what it's intended for (which is clearing out stuffy heads). Pseudo-ephedrine is a *stimulant*. This means it makes your heart beat faster and raises your blood pressure. It can make you feel excited and "hyped up." Athletes sometimes abuse pseudoephedrine to help them get "pumped" before a big game. People also sometimes use pseudoephedrine to lose weight. But taking pseudoephedrine for non-medicinal uses can be dangerous, especially if people take more than the recommended dose.

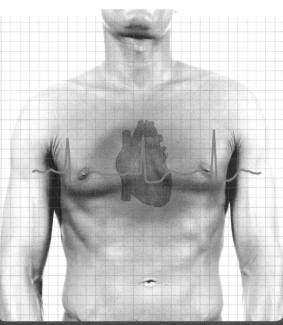

Abusing pseudoephedrine can cause heart palpitations, irregular heart rhythms, or even heart attacks.

Because pseudoephedrine is one of the ingredients used to "cook" meth, new laws in the United States now require that any medication containing pseudoephedrine be kept behind the pharmacy counter. People still don't need a doctor's prescription to buy it, but they will need to show identification, and they will be limited to a certain amount of the medication per month.

8. WHAT HAPPENS TO YOUR BODY WHEN YOU USE LAXATIVES?

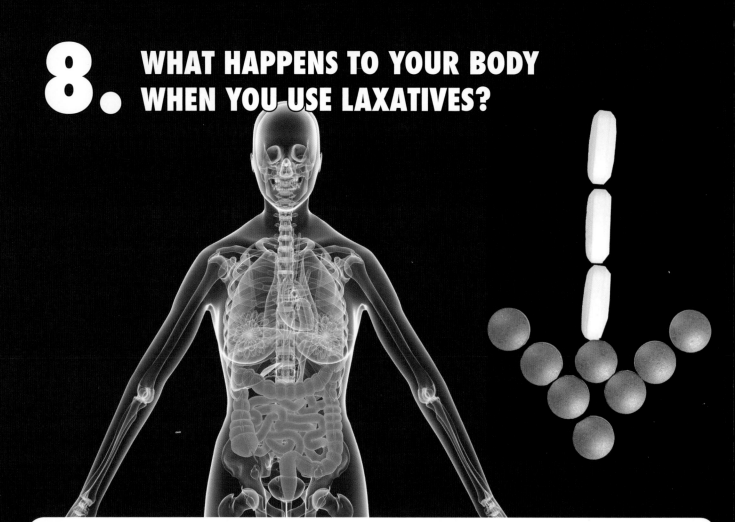

Teenagers and adults sometimes abuse laxatives as a way to try to lose weight. Laxatives make your bowels move more often; in other words, they make you poop. People think that if the laxatives rush the food through their stomachs and intestines, their bodies won't have time to absorb calories from their food. But that's not the way the intestines work. By the time laxatives act on the large intestine, most foods and calories have already been absorbed inside the small intestine. Although laxatives make the large intestine empty itself faster, losing water, *minerals*, *electrolytes*, and *fiber* is what causes the only weight loss. The body needs all these things to work correctly—and the weight will usually come back as soon as the person drinks something.

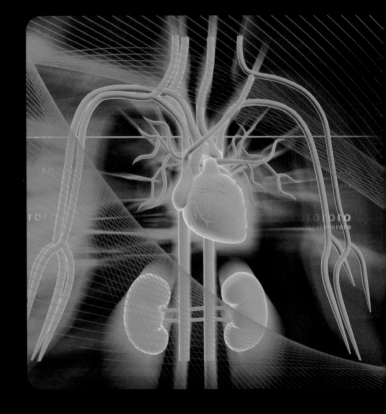

Abusing laxatives can cause **dehydration**. Your body's organs need water in order to do their jobs. Dehydration can damage them. Severe dehydration can cause tremors, weakness, blurry vision, fainting, kidney damage, and even death. Dehydration often requires medical treatment.

Using laxatives too often can throw your body's electrolytes and minerals out of balance. Your nerves and muscles (including the muscles of your heart) need specific amounts of minerals like sodium, potassium, magnesium, and phosphorus to work correctly. Upsetting the balance of these minerals can make your organs shut down.

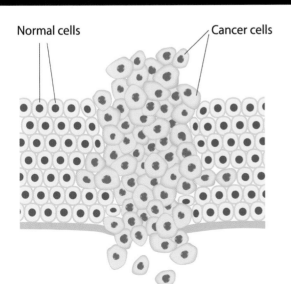

Normal cells   Cancer cells

If you abuse laxatives, your large intestine can come to depend on them in order to work. (So you won't be able to go to the bathroom anymore without taking laxatives.) Your large intestine may be damaged by laxative abuse. Laxatives may also make you more at risk for getting colon cancer.

9. WHAT HAPPENS TO YOUR BODY WHEN YOU USE HERBAL DRUGS?

Teenagers and adults take herbal medications for all sorts of reasons. They take them to lose weight, to treat illnesses, and even to get high. Many times they think that "herbal" equals "safe." They believe that because these substances come from plants and other natural substances, they can't be dangerous. But these substances can actually be very dangerous.

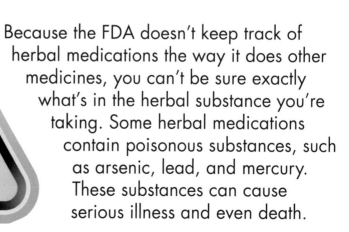

Because the FDA doesn't keep track of herbal medications the way it does other medicines, you can't be sure exactly what's in the herbal substance you're taking. Some herbal medications contain poisonous substances, such as arsenic, lead, and mercury. These substances can cause serious illness and even death.

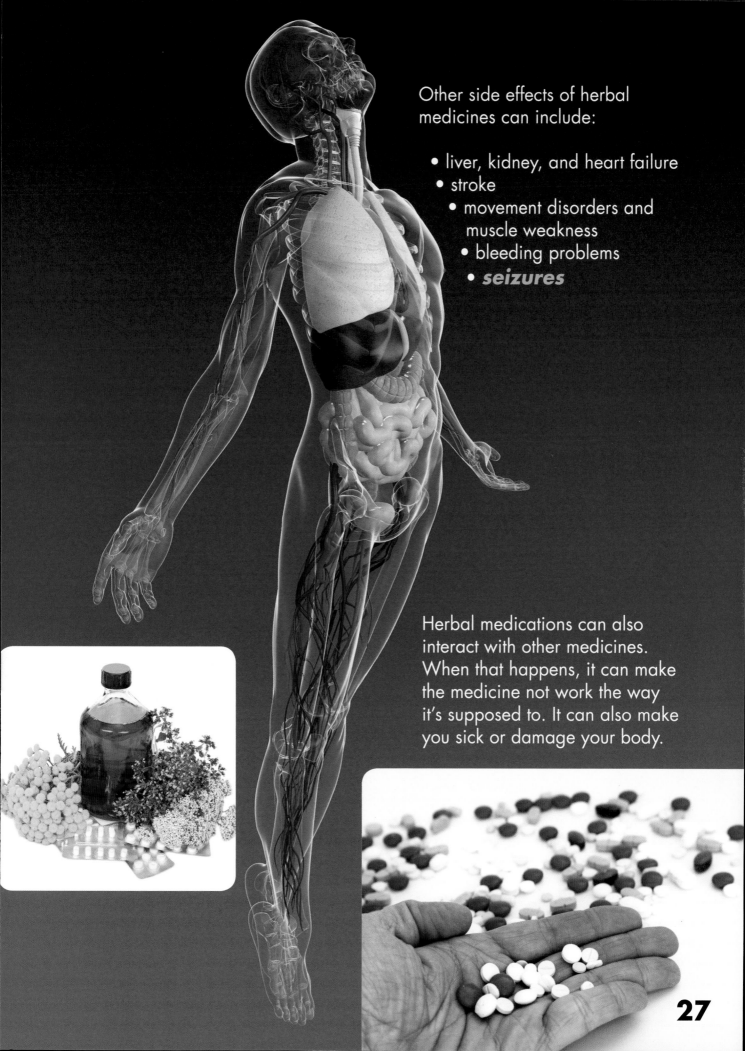

Other side effects of herbal medicines can include:

- liver, kidney, and heart failure
- stroke
- movement disorders and muscle weakness
- bleeding problems
- *seizures*

Herbal medications can also interact with other medicines. When that happens, it can make the medicine not work the way it's supposed to. It can also make you sick or damage your body.

10. WHAT DOES DXM DO TO YOUR BRAIN?

The greater the dose of DXM, the more it affects the brain. DXM changes the way neurotransmitters work inside your brain. Neurotransmitters carry messages between your nerve cells. By changing them, DXM can make people feel happy and dreamy—or "high." At great enough doses, DXM makes you hallucinate. In other words, you'll start seeing or hearing things that aren't really there.

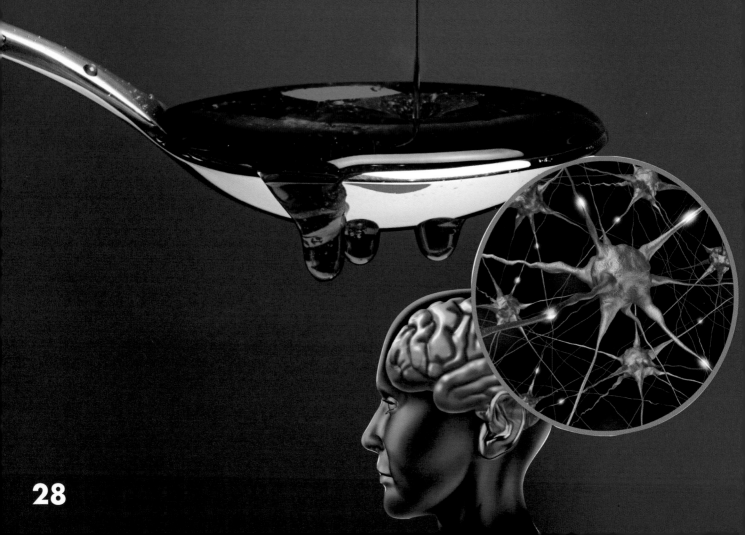

DXM can block your brain's ability to send messages to the rest of your body, so you may not be able to move or see normally. In 2003, a fourteen-year-old boy who abused DXM died when two cars hit him as he tried to cross a highway. Investigators believe that taking DXM affected his depth perception and caused him to misjudge the distance and speed of the oncoming vehicles.

DXM can interfere with your brain's memory and decision-making abilities.

Long-term DXM abuse may cause permanent brain damage.

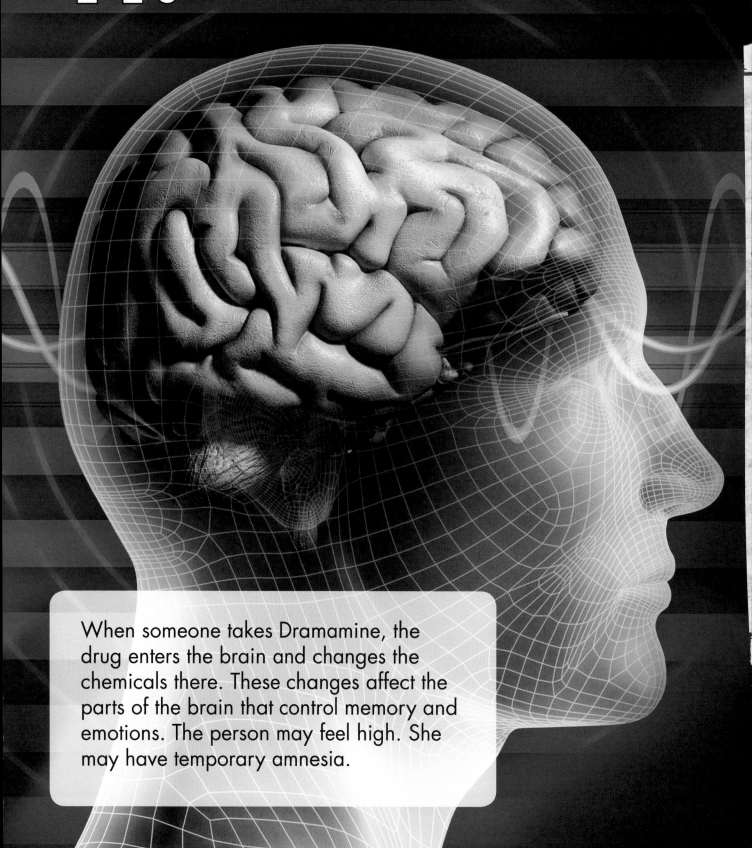

When someone takes Dramamine, the drug enters the brain and changes the chemicals there. These changes affect the parts of the brain that control memory and emotions. The person may feel high. She may have temporary amnesia.

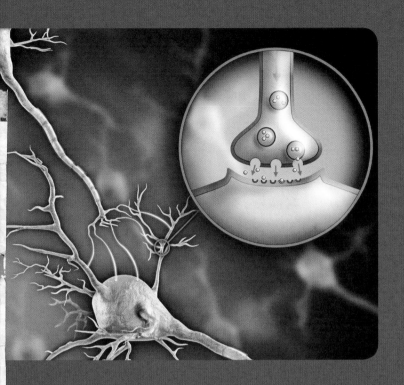

Dramamine acts on a powerful neurotransmitter found in the brain called acetylcholine. Normally, acetylcholine works in many different sites in the brain—but when Dramamine is present, acetylcholine can't carry its messages between nerve cells the way it usually would. Many of the nerves that have to do with your stomach and digestion are activated by acetylcholine, so this is how Dramamine keeps people from getting sick to their stomachs. But the changes in acetylcholine levels in the brain can also cause strange dreams and confusion, even at low levels.

At higher levels, the person can start to hallucinate. He could even lose consciousness.

Many diet pills work by tricking the body into believing that it's not hungry. They affect the brain chemicals that control appetite and interfere with the hunger signals the brain normally sends out to the rest of the body when it needs food.

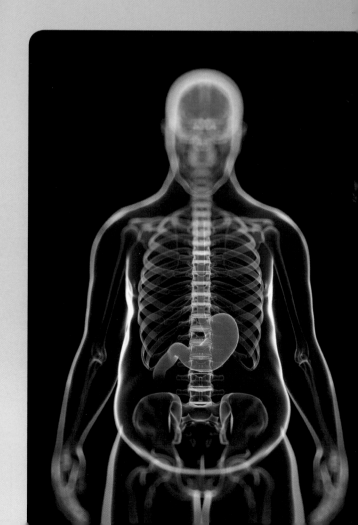

Stress
Stress
Stress
Stress

Many diet pills also contain caffeine or other chemicals that *stimulate* your brain to send messages to the glands in your body that make adrenaline. Adrenaline is the chemical that's released when you're scared or nervous. It's meant to help you deal with danger—but too much adrenaline in your system will make you feel stressed out. It's hard on you emotionally to feel like that all the time. It can cause *depression* and *anxiety*, both of which can become serious psychiatric disorders. That stressed-out feeling isn't good for your body either!

Remember, the best way to lose weight is always healthy diet and exercise. There's no magic pill you can take to make you lose weight!

13. WHAT DO SLEEPING PILLS DO TO YOUR BRAIN?

The antihistamines found in many over-the-counter sleeping pills are meant to block allergic reactions. By doing that, they also trigger the parts of your brain that make you sleepy.

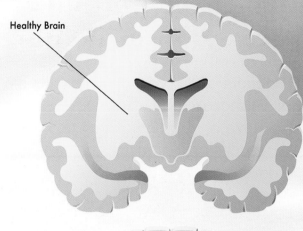

Healthy Brain

Sleeping pills slow down your brain's reactions.

Some *research* indicates that using antihistamines (the chemical in most OTC sleeping pills) too much could cause brain cancer.

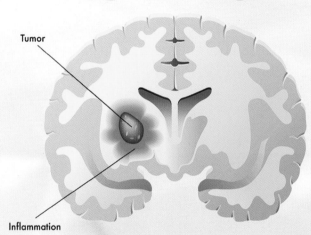

Tumor

Inflammation

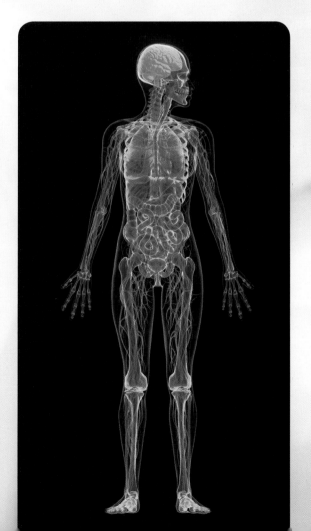

Sleeping pills can affect the parts of your brain you use to think and make decisions.

The chemicals in sleeping pills can interfere with your brain's ability to send out messages to the rest of your body. This can mean you can't move normally.

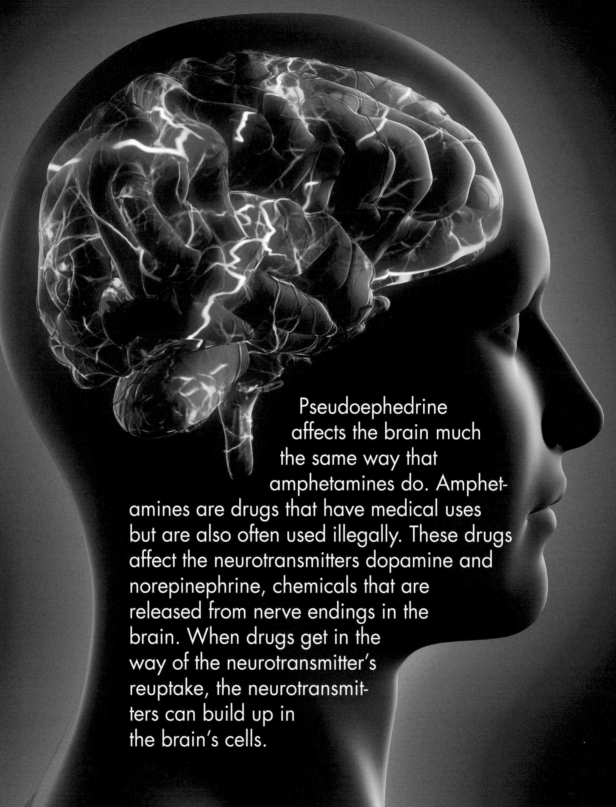

WHAT DOES PSEUDOEPHEDRINE DO TO YOUR BRAIN?

Pseudoephedrine affects the brain much the same way that amphetamines do. Amphetamines are drugs that have medical uses but are also often used illegally. These drugs affect the neurotransmitters dopamine and norepinephrine, chemicals that are released from nerve endings in the brain. When drugs get in the way of the neurotransmitter's reuptake, the neurotransmitters can build up in the brain's cells.

Dopamine has a role to play in these brain functions:

- memory
- sense of pleasure
- thinking
- judgment
- attention
- sleep
- mood
- learning

Using pseudoephedrine can interfere with all these!

Norepinephrine also affects attention and mood. It regulates the fight-or-flight response, which is how your brain prepares you to handle danger. When there's too much of this chemical in your brain, you can feel stressed and anxious.

15. WHAT DO LAXATIVES AND HERBAL DRUGS DO TO YOUR BRAIN?

Because laxatives pull water from your body, they can interfere with your brain's function. Like all the other cells in your body, your brain cells need water to be healthy.

Even mild dehydration can change the chemicals in your brain. This can affect your mood (making you more likely to feel sad or angry or worried). It can also make it hard for you to think clearly.

Because there are so many different kinds of herbal drugs, there are many ways they can affect your brain. Some herbal medications can change your mood. Others can make you hallucinate. When you're taking herbal drugs, it's hard to know what to expect!

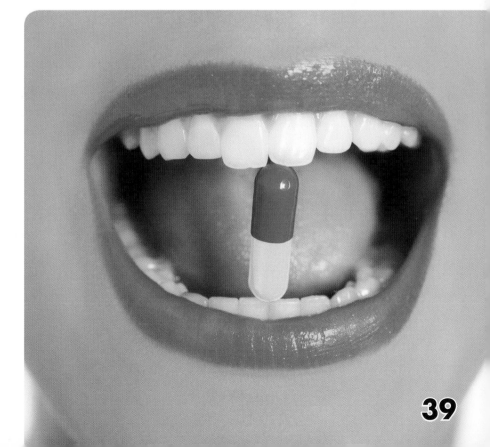

16. MORE QUESTIONS?

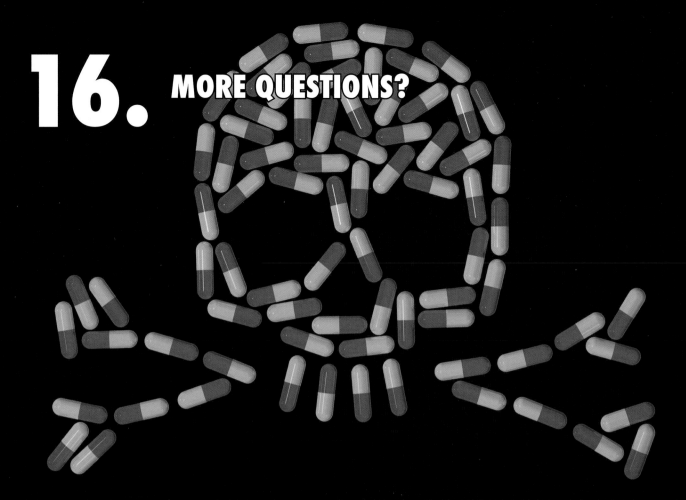

Who abuses over-the-counter drugs?

Teenagers are among those who most often abuse OTC. This may be because teens can get these drugs so easily—and also because they may not understand that these drugs can be very dangerous. In any case, they've become very popular with kids between thirteen and sixteen years old. One out of every ten teens reports using DXM to get high. Hospitals have treated many overdoses from these drugs in this age group.

What happens if you combine over-the-counter drugs?

When you combine OTC drugs, they can become even more dangerous. The chemicals in them can interact with each other, which means they may produce new reactions inside your body and brain. Some of these reactions could even be deadly.

...at should I do if I or someone I know has a problem
...n over-the-counter drugs?

...first step is to talk to a doctor, a school counselor, your parents,
...her adult you trust. Whomever you talk to, the next step will pro...
... be to consult with a doctor. She will be able to tell you what to
.... Don't put off taking the first step! OTC drugs can be dangerous...

FURTHER READING

Brown, Rani L. *But Is It Safe?* New York: Blue Lotus, 2012.

Dasgupta, Amitava. *Prescription or Poison? The Benefits and Dangers of Herbal Remedies*. Newport, R.I.: Hunter House, 2010.

Kuhar, Michael. *The Addicted Brain*. Upper Saddle River, N.J.: FT Press Science, 2011.

Kuhn, Cynthia. *Buzzed: The Straight Facts About the Most Used and Abused Drugs*. New York: Norton, 2008.

Shaw, Brian F. *Addiction and Recovery for Dummies*. Hoboken, N.J.: For Dummies, 2004.

FIND OUT MORE ON THE INTERNET

Dangers of Buying Medicines Over the Internet
www.fda.gov/forconsumers/consumerupdates/ucm048396.htm

Drug Facts: Prescription and Over-the-Counter Drugs
www.drugabuse.gov/publications/drugfacts/prescription-over-counter-medications

OTC Medications: Understanding the Risks
www.urmc.rochester.edu/encyclopedia/
content.aspx?ContentTypeID=1&ContentID=4531

OTC Medicines: Know Your Risks
familydoctor.org/familydoctor/en/drugs-procedures-devices/
over-the-counter/otc-medicines-know-your-risks-and-reduce-them.html

Over-the-Counter Drugs
www.abovetheinfluence.com/facts/drugsotc

NIDA for Teens
teens.drugabuse.gov/peerx/facts-rx-and-over-counter-drugs

Seven Very Dangerous Over-the-Counter Drugs
fmcfsme.com/7dangerousotcmeds.php

Stop Medicine Abuse
stopmedicineabuse.org/what-does-abuse-look-like

GLOSSARY

anxiety: A feeling of worry or unease.

beneficial: Good for you.

chemical: A substance that has been purified or prepared.

coma: Deep unconsciousness from which a person can't wake up.

convulsions: Sudden, violent movements of your muscles.

dehydration: When your body doesn't have enough water to function correctly.

depression: A long-lasting feeling of sadness and hopelessness.

electrolytes: Substances in your body that help your nerves and muscles work correctly and help balance how much water is in your cells.

fiber: Tough, indigestable plant matter that helps you digest food normally.

glands: The organs where certain substances are made in your body.

illicit: Against the law.

impaired: Having your abilities damaged in some way.

metabolism: The process by which your body breaks down food and other chemicals.

minerals: Solid materials found in nature, such as iron or copper. Your body needs certain minerals in very small quantities.

prescription: A note from a doctor instructing you to take a certain drug. You need a prescription to get many drugs.

research: In-depth study of new things (such as drugs) to learn more about them.

seizures: Unusual electrical activity in the brain that can result in unconsciousness and convulsions.

sensitive: Having a strong reaction to a drug or other stimulus.

stimulant: A drug that makes your body work faster or harder in some way. It might make you feel more energetic or awake.

stimulate: Raise levels of activity in a certain part of the body.

stroke: A blocked or burst blood vessel in your brain, which may cause brain damage.

withdrawal: The negative effects you feel when you stop taking a drug that you're dependent on.

INDEX

PICTURE CREDITS

ABOUT THE AUTHOR
AND THE CONSULTANT

ROSA WATERS lives in New York State. She has worked as a writer for several years, producing works on health, history, and other topics.

DR. JOSHUA BORUS, MD, MPH, graduated from the Harvard Medical School and the Harvard School of Public Health. He completed a residency in pediatrics and then served as chief resident at Floating Hospital for Children at Tufts Medical Center before completing a fellowship in Adolescent Medicine at Boston Children's Hospital. He is currently an attending physician in the Division of Adolescent and Young Adult Medicine at Boston Children's Hospital and an instructor of pediatrics at Harvard Medical School.